Shamar's War

by

Kris Neville

Shamar's War
by Kris Neville

Copyright © 2023

All Rights reserved.

No part of this publication may be reproduced, stored in a retrieval system, or transmitted in any form or by any means, electronic, mechanical, photocopying or Otherwise, without the written permission of the publisher.
The author/editor asserts the moral right to be identified as the author/editor of this work.

ISBN: 978-93-59322-57-5

Published by

DOUBLE 9 BOOKS

2/13-B, Ansari Road
Daryaganj, New Delhi – 110002
info@double9books.com
www.double9books.com
Tel. 011-40042856

ABOUT THE AUTHOR

Kris Ottman Neville (May 9, 1925 – December 23, 1980) was a California-based American science fiction writer. He was born in the city of St. Louis. His debut work of science fiction was published in 1949. His most renowned work, the novella Bettyann, is regarded as a science fiction classic. The following biographical note about Kris Neville was written by well-known science fiction writer and critic Barry N. Malzberg in his introduction to Neville's story Ballenger's People in the 1979 Doubleday anthology Neglected Visions: Kris Neville could have been one of the ten most honored science fiction writers of his generation; instead, after conquering the field early on, he virtually abandoned it and established himself as the world's leading lay authority on epoxy resins, collaborating on a series of specialized texts that have become standard works in their field. I can't blame him for making this decision, which was clearly well thought out. Neville, who sold his first story in 1949 and fifteen more by 1952, realized early on that the boundaries of the field in the 1950s were simply too close to contain the kind of work he would have to undertake if he wanted to progress as a writer, and he quit.

CONTENTS

CHAPTER I

The year was 2346, and Earth, at the time, was a political democracy.

The population was ruled by the Over-Council and, in order of decreasing importance, by Councils, and Local Councils. Each was composed of representatives duly apportioned by popular vote between the two contending parties. Executive direction was provided by a variety of Secretaries, selected by vote of the appropriate Councils. An independent Judiciary upheld the laws.

A unified Earth sent colonists to the stars. Back came strange tales and improbable animals.

Back, too, came word of a burgeoning technological civilization on the planet Itra, peopled by entirely humanoid aliens.

Earth felt it would be wise for Itra to join in a Galactic Federation and accordingly, submitted the terms of such a mutually advantageous agreement.

The Itraians declined....

Space Captain Merle S. Shaeffer, the youngest and perhaps the most naive pilot for Trans-Universe Transport, was called unexpectedly to the New York office of the company.

When Capt. Shaeffer entered the luxurious eightieth story suite, Old Tom Twilmaker, the President of TUT, greeted him. With an arm around his shoulder, Old Tom led Capt. Shaeffer to an immense inner office and introduced him to a General Reuter, identified as the Chairman of the Interscience Committee of the Over-Council.

No one else was present. With the door closed, they were isolated in Olympian splendor above and beyond the affairs of men. Here judgments were final and impartial. Capt. Shaeffer, in the presence of two of the men highest in the ruling councils of Earth, was reduced to incoherent awe.

General Reuter moved about restlessly. Old Tom was serene and beatific.

When they were seated, Old Tom swiveled around and gazed long in silence across the spires of the City. Capt. Shaeffer waited respectfully. General Reuter fidgetted.

"Some day," Old Tom said at last, "I'm going to take my leave of this. Yes, gentle Jesus! Oh, when I think of all the souls still refusing to admit our precious Savior, what bitterness, oh, what sorrow is my wealth to me! Look down upon the teeming millions below us. How many know not the Lord? Yes, some morning, I will forsake all this and go out into the streets to spend my last days bringing the words of hope to the weary and oppressed. Are you a Christian, Merle?"

General Reuter cracked his knuckles nervously while Capt. Shaeffer muttered an embarrassed affirmative.

"I am a deeply religious man," Old Tom continued. "I guess you've heard that, Merle?"

"Yes sir," Capt. Shaeffer said.

"But did you know that the Lord has summoned you here today?" Old Tom asked.

"No, sir," Capt. Shaeffer said.

"General Reuter, here, is a dear friend. We've known each other, oh, many years. Distantly related through our dear wives, in fact. And we serve on the same Board of Directors and the same Charity Committees.... A few weeks ago, when he asked me for a man, I called for your file, Merle. I made discreet inquiries. Then I got down on my knees and talked it over with God for, oh, it must have been all of an hour. I asked, 'Is this the man?' And I was given a sign. Yes! At that moment, a shaft of sunlight broke through the clouds!"

General Reuter had continued his nervous movements throughout the speech. For the first time, he spoke. "Good God, Tom, serve us a drink." He turned to Capt. Shaeffer. "A little drink now and then helps a man relax. I'll just have mine straight, Tom."

Old Tom studied Capt. Shaeffer. "I do not feel the gentle Master approves of liquor."

"Don't try to influence him," General Reuter said. "You're embarrassing the boy."

"I—" Capt. Shaeffer began.

"Give him the drink. If he doesn't want to drink it, he won't have to drink it."

Sighing, Old Tom poured two bourbons from the bar in back of his desk and passed them over. Martyrdom sat heavily upon his brow.

After a quick twist of the wrist and an expert toss of the head, General Reuter returned an empty glass. "Don't mind if I do have another," he said. He was already less restless.

"How's your ability to pick up languages?" General Reuter asked.

"I learned Spanish and Russian at TUT PS," Capt. Shaeffer said apologetically. "I'm supposed to have a real high aptitude in languages, according to some tests I took. In case we should meet intelligent aliens, TUT gives them."

"You got no association with crackpot organizations, anything like that?" General Reuter asked. "You're either a good Liberal-Conservative or Radical-Progressive, aren't you? I don't care which. I don't believe in prying into a man's politics."

"I never belonged to anything," Capt. Shaeffer said.

"Oh, I can assure you, that's been checked out very, very thoroughly," Old Tom said.

The General signaled for another drink. With a sigh of exasperation, Old Tom complied.

"Bob," Old Tom said, "I really think you've had enough. Please, now. Our Master counsels moderation."

"Damn it, Tom," the General said and turned back to the space pilot. "May have a little job for you."

Old Tom shook his head at the General, cautioning him.

"Actually," the General said, ignoring the executive, "we'll be sort of renting you from TUT. In a way you'll still be working for them. I can get a million dollars out of the—"

"Bob!"

"—unmarked appropriation if it goes in in TUT's name. No questions asked. National Defense. I couldn't get anywhere near that much for an individual for a year. It gives us a pie to slice. We were talking about it before you came in. How does a quarter of a million dollars a year sound to you?"

"When it comes to such matters," Old Tom interjected hastily, "I think first of the opportunities they bring to do good."

The General continued, "Now you know, Merle. And this is serious. I want you to listen to me. Because this comes under World Security laws, and I'm going to bind you to them. You know what that means? You'll be held responsible."

"Yes, sir," Merle said, swallowing stiffly. "I understand."

"Good. Let's have a drink on that."

"Please be quiet, General," Old Tom said. "Let me explain. You see, Merle, the Interscience Committee was recently directed to consider methods for creating a climate of opinion on Itra—of which I'm sure you've heard—which would be favorable to the proposed Galactic Federation."

"Excuse me," General Reuter said. "They don't have a democracy, like we do. They don't have any freedom like we do. I have no doubt the average whateveryoucallem—Itraians, I guess—the average gooks—would be glad to see us come in and just kick the hell out of whoever is in charge of them."

"Now, General," Old Tom said more sharply.

"But that's not the whole thing," the General continued. "Even fit were right thing to do, an' I'm not saying isn't—right thing to do—there's log-lo-lo-gistics. I don't want to convey the impresh, impression that our Defense Force people have been wasting money. Never had as much as needed, fact. No, it's like this.

"We have this broad base to buil' from. Backbone. But we live in a democracy. Now, Old Tom's Liberal-Conservative. And me, I'm Radical-Progresshive. But we agree on one thing: importance of strong defense. A lot of people don' understan' this. Feel we're already spendin' more than we can afford. But I want to ask them, what's more important than the defense of our planet?"

"General, I'm afraid this is not entirely germane," Old Tom said stiffly.

"Never mind that right now. Point is, it will take us long time to get the serious nature of the menace of Itra across to the voters. Then, maybe fifteen, twenty years.... Let's just take one thing. We don't have anywhere near enough troop transports to carry out the occupation of Itra. You know how long it takes to build them? My point is, we may not have that long. Suppose Itra should get secret of interstellar drive tomorrow, then where would we be?"

Old Tom slammed his fist on the desk. "General, please! The boy isn't interested in all that."

The General surged angrily to his feet. "By God, that's what's wrong with this world today!" he cried. "Nobody's interested in Defense. Spend only a measly twenty per cent of the Gross World Product on Defense, and expect to keep strong! Good God, Tom, give me a drink!" Apparently heresy had shocked him sober.

Old Tom explained, "The General is a patriot. We all respect him for it."

"I understand," Capt. Shaeffer said.

General Reuter hammered his knuckles in rhythm on the table. "The drink, the drink, the drink! You got more in the bottle. I saw it!"

Old Tom rolled his eyes Heavenward and passed the bottle across. "This is all you get. This is all I've got."

The General held the bottle up to the light. "Should have brought my own. Let's hurry up and get this over with."

Old Tom smiled the smile of the sorely beset and persecuted and said, "You see, Merle, there's massive discontent among the population of Itra. We feel we should send a man to the planet to, well, foment change and, uh, hasten the already inevitable overthrow of the despotic government. That man will be strictly on his own. The Government will not be able to back him in any way whatsoever once he lands on Itra."

The General had quickly finished the bottle. "You she," he interrupted, "there's one thing they can't fight, an' that's an idea. Jus' one man goes to Itra with the idea of Freedom, that's all it'll take. How many men did it take to start the 'Merican Revolution? Jefferson. The Russian Revolution? Marx!"

"Yes," Old Tom said. "One dedicated man on Itra, preaching the ideas of Liberty—liberty with responsibility and property rights under one God. That man can change a world." Exhausted by the purity of his emotions, Old Tom sat back gasping to await the answer.

"A quarter of a million dollars a year?" Capt. Shaeffer asked at length.

CHAPTER II

The Itraians spoke a common language. It was somewhat guttural and highly inflected. Fortunately, the spelling appeared to be phonetic, with only forty-three characters being required. As near as anyone could tell, centuries of worldwide communication had eliminated regional peculiarities. The speech from one part of Itra was not distinguishable from that of another part.

Most of the language was recovered from spy tapes of television programs. A dictionary was compiled laborously by a special scientific task force of the Over-Council. The overall program was directed and administered by Intercontinental Iron, Steel, Gas, Electricity, Automobiles and Synthetics, Incorporated.

It took Shaeffer just short of three years to speak Itraian sufficiently well to convince non-Itraians that he spoke without accent.

The remainder of his training program was administered by a variety of other large industrial concerns. The training was conducted at a Defense Facility.

At the end of his training, Shaeffer was taken by special bus to the New Mexican space port. A ship waited.

The car moved smoothly from the Defense Force Base, down the broad sixteen-lane highway, through the surrounding slum area and into Grants.

Sight of the slums gave Shaeffer mixed emotions.

It was not a feeling of superiority to the inhabitants; those he had always regarded with a circumspect indifference. The slums were there. He supposed they always would be there. But now, for the first time in his life, he could truly say that he had escaped their omnipresent threat once and for all. He felt relief and guilt.

During the last three years, he had earned $750,000.

As a civilian stationed on a Defense Force Base, he had, of course, to pay for his clothing, his food and his lodging. But the charge was nominal. Since he had been given only infrequent and closely supervised leaves, he had been able to spend, altogether, only $12,000.

Which meant that now, after taxes, he had accumulated in his savings account a total of nearly $600,000 awaiting his return from Itra.

Shaeffer's ship stood off Itra while he prepared to disembark.

In his cramped quarters, he dressed himself in Itraian-style clothing. Capt. Merle S. Shaeffer became Shamar the Worker.

In addition to his jump equipment, an oxygen cylinder, a face mask and a shovel, he carried with him eighty pounds of counterfeit Itraian currency ... all told, forty thousand individual bills of various denominations. Earth felt this would be all he needed to survive in a technologically advanced civilization.

His plan was as follows:

1. He was to land in a sparsely inhabited area on the larger masses.

2. He was to procure transportation to Xxla, a major city, equivalent to London or Tokyo. It was the headquarters for the Party.

3. He was to establish residence in the slum area surrounding the University of Xxla.

4. Working through student contacts, he was to ingratiate himself with such rebel intellectuals as could be found.

5. Once his contacts were secure, he was to assist in the preparation of propaganda and establish a clandestine press for its production.

6. As quickly as the operation was self-sufficient, he was to move on to another major city ... and begin all over.

The ship descended into the atmosphere. The bell rang. Shamar the Worker seated himself, put on his oxygen mask and signaled his readiness. He breathed oxygen. The ship quivered, the door fell away beneath him and he was battered unconscious by the slipstream.

Five minutes later, pinwheeling lazily in free fall, he opened his eyes. For an instant's panic he could not read the altimeter. Then seeing that he was safe, he noted his physical sensations. He was extremely cold. Gyrating wildly, he beat his chest to restore circulation.

He stabilized his fall by stretching out his hands. He floated with no sensation of movement. Itra was overhead, falling up at him slowly. He turned his back to the planet and checked the time. Twelve minutes yet to go.

He spent, in all, seventeen minutes in free fall. At 2000 feet, he opened his parachute. The sound was like an explosion.

He floated quietly, recovering from the shock. He removed his oxygen mask and tasted the alien air. He sniffed several times. It was not unpleasant.

Below was darkness. Then suddenly the ground came floating up and hit him.

The terrain was irregular. He fought the chute to collapse it, tripped, and twisted his ankle painfully.

The chute lay quiet and he sat on the ground and cursed in English.

At length he bundled up the chute and removed all of the packages of money but the one disguised as a field pack. He used the shovel to dig a shallow grave at the base of a tree. He interred the chute, the oxygen cylinder, the mask, the shovel and scooped dirt over them with his hands.

He sat down and unlaced his shoe and found his ankle badly swollen. Distant, unfamiliar odors filled him with apprehension and he started at the slightest sound.

Dawn was breaking.

CHAPTER III

Noting his bearings carefully, he hobbled painfully westward, with thirty pounds of money on his back. He would intersect the major North-South Intercontinental highway by at least noon.

Two hours later, he came to a small plastic cabin in a clearing at the edge of a forest.

Wincing now with each step, he made his way to the door. He knocked.

There was a long wait.

The door opened. A girl stood before him in a dressing gown. She frowned and asked, *"Itsil obwatly jer gekompilp?"*

Hearing Itraian spoken by a native in the flesh had a powerful emotional impact on Shamar the Worker.

Stumblingly, he introduced himself and explained that he was camping out. During the previous night he had become lost and injured his ankle. If she could spare him food and directions, he would gladly pay.

With a smile of superiority, she stepped aside and said in Itraian, "Come in, Chom the Worker."

He felt panic, but he choked it back and followed her. Apparently he had horribly mispronounced his own name. It was as though, in English he had said Barchestershire for Barset. He cursed whatever Professor had picked that name for whatever obscure reason.

"Sit down," she invited. "I'm about to have breakfast. Eggs and bacon—" the Itraian equivalent—"if that's all right with you. I'm Garfling Germadpoldlt by the way, although you can call me Ge-Ge."

The food was quite unpleasant, as though overly ripe. He was able to choke down the eggs with the greatest difficulty. Fortunately, the hot drink that was the equivalent of Earth coffee at the end of the meal, was sufficiently spicy to quiet his stomach.

"Good coffee," he said.

"Thank you. Care for a cigarette?"

"I sure would."

He had no matches, so she lit it for him, hovering above him a moment, leaving with him the fresh odor of her hair.

The taste of the cigarette was mild. Rather surprisingly, it substituted for nicotine and allayed the sharp longing that had come with the coffee.

"Let's look at your ankle," she said. She knelt at his feet and began to unlace the right shoe. "My, it's swollen," she said sympathetically.

He winced as she touched it and then he reddened with embarrassment. He had been walking across dusty country. He drew back the foot and bent to restrain her.

Playfully she slapped his hand away. "You sit back! I'll get it. I've seen dirty feet before."

She pulled off the shoe and peeled off the sock. "Oh, God, it is swollen," she said. "You think it's broken, Shamar?"

"Just sprained."

"I'll get some hot water with some MedAid in it, and that'll take the swelling out."

When he had his foot in the water, she sat across from him and arranged her dressing gown with a coquettish gesture. She caught him staring at the earring, and one hand went to it caressingly. She smiled that universal feminine smile of security and recklessness, of invitation and rejection.

"You're engaged," he noted.

She opened her eyes wide and studied him above a thumbnail which she tasted with her teeth. "I'm engaged to Von Stutsman—" as the name might be translated—"perhaps you've heard of him? He's important in the Party. You know him?"

"No."

"You in the Party?" she said. She was teasing him now. Then, suddenly: "Neither am I, but I guess I'll have to join if I become Mrs. Von Stutsman."

They were silent for a moment.

Then she spoke, and he was frozen in terror, all thoughts but of self-preservation washed from his mind.

"Your accent is unbelieveably bad," she said.

"I'm from Zuleb," he said lamely, at last.

"Meta—Gelwhops—or even Karkeqwol, that makes no difference. Nobody on Itra speaks like you do. So you must be from that planet that had the Party in a flap several years ago—Earth, isn't it?"

He said nothing.

"Do you know what they'll do when they catch you?" she asked.

"No," he said hollowly.

"They'll behead you."

She laughed, not unkindly. "If you could see yourself! How ridiculous you look, Shamar. I wonder what your real name is, by the way? Sitting with a foot in the water and looking wildly about. Here, let me fix more coffee and we can talk."

She called cheerily over her shoulder, "You're safe here. No one will be by. I'm not due back until Tuesday."

She brought him a steaming mug. "Drink this while I dress." She disappeared into the bedroom. He heard the shower running.

He sat waiting, numb and desperate, and drank the coffee because it was there. His thoughts scampered in the cage of his skull like mice on a treadmill.

When Ge-Ge came back, he had still not resolved the conflict within him. She stood barefoot upon the rug and looked down at him, hunched miserably over the pan of water, now lukewarm.

"How's the foot?"

"All right."

"Want to take it out?"

"I guess."

"I'll get a towel."

She waited until he had dried the foot and restored the sock and shoe. The swelling was gone. He stood up and put his weight on it. He smiled wanly. "It's okay now. It's not broken, I guess."

She gestured him to the sofa. He complied.

"What's in the field pack?" she asked. "Money? How much?" She moved toward it. He half rose to stop her, but by then she had it partly open. "My," she said, bringing out a thick sheaf of bills. She rippled them sensuously. "Pretty. Very, very pretty." She examined them for texture and appearance. "They look good, Shamar. I'll bet it would cost ten million dollars in research on paper and ink and presses to do this kind of a job. Only another government has got that kind of money to throw around." She tossed the currency carelessly beside him and came to sit at his side.

She took his hand. Her hand was warm and gentle. "Tell me, Shamar," she said. "Tell me all about it."

So this is how easily spies are trapped in real life, Shamar told himself with numb disbelief.

The story came out slowly and hesitantly at first. She said nothing until he had finished.

"And that's all? You really believe that, don't you? And I guess your government does, too. That all we need is just some little idea or something." She turned away from him. "But of course, that's neither here nor there, is it? I never imagined an adventurer type would look like you. You have such a soft, honest voice. As a little girl, I pictured myself being carried off by a tanned desert sheik on a camel; and oh, he was lean and handsome! With dark flashing eyes and murderously heavy lips and hands like iron! Well, that's life, I guess." She stood and paced the room. "Let me think. We'll pick up a flyer in Zelonip when we catch the bus next Tuesday. How much does the money weigh?"

"Eighty pounds."

"I can carry about 10 pounds in my bag. You can take your field pack. How much is in it? Thirty pounds? That'll leave about forty which we can ship through on extra charges. Then, when we get to Xxla, I can hide you out in an apartment over on the East side."

"Why would you run a risk like that for me?" he asked.

She brushed the hair from her face. "Let's say—what? I don't really think you can make it, because it's so hopeless. But maybe, just maybe, you might be one of the rare ones who, if he plays his cards right, can beat the system. I love to see them licked!

"Well, I'm a clerk. That's all. Just a lowly clerk in one of the Party offices. I met Von Stutsman a year ago. This is his cabin. He lets me use it.

"He's older than I am; but there's worse husband material. But then again, he's about to be transferred to one of the big agricultural combines way out in the boondocks where there's no excitement at all. Just little old ladies and little old men and peasants having children.

"I'm a city girl. I like Xxla. And if I marry him, all that goes up the flue. I'll be marooned with him, God knows where, for years. Stuck, just stuck.

"Still—he is Von Stutsman, and he's on his way up. Everyone says that. Ten, twenty years, he'll be back to Xxla, and he'll come back on top.

"Oh ... I don't know what I want to do! If I marry him, I can get all the things I've always wanted. Position, security. He's older than I am, but he's really a nice guy. It's just that he's dull. He can't talk about anything but Party, Party, Party.

"That's what I came out to this cabin for. To think things over, to try to get things straightened out. And then you came along. Maybe it gives me a chance for something exciting before I ship off to the boondocks. Does that make sense to you?

"I'll get married and sit out there, and I'll turn the pages of the Party magazine and smile sweetly to myself. Because, you see, I'll always be able to lean forward and say, 'Dear? Once upon a time, I helped hide an Earth spy in Xxla.' And that'll knock that silly and self-satisfied look off his face for once.... Oh, I don't know! Let me alone!" With that, she fled to the bedroom and slammed the door behind her.

He could hear her sobbing helplessly.

In the afternoon, she came out. He had fallen asleep. She shook him gently to waken him.

"Eh? Oh! Huh?" He smiled foolishly.

"Wash up in there," she told him. "I'm sorry I blew up on you this morning. I'll cook something."

When he came back, she was serving them their dinner on steaming platters.

"Look, Ge-Ge," he said over coffee. "You don't like your government. We'll help you out. There's this Galactic Federation idea." He explained to her the cross-fertilization of the two cultures.

"Shamar, my friend," she said, "did you see Earth's proposal? There was nothing in it about giving us an interstellar drive. We were required to give Earth all transportation franchises. The organization you used to work for was to be given, as I remember it, an exclusive ninety-nine year right to carry all Earth-Itra commerce. It was all covered in the newspapers, didn't you see it?"

Shamar said, "Well, now, I'm not familiar with the details. I wasn't keeping up with them. But I'm sure these things could be, you know, worked out. Maybe, for Security reasons, we didn't want to give you the interstellar drive right off, but you can appreciate our logic there. Once we saw you were, well, like us, a peace-loving planet, once you'd changed your government to a democracy, you would see it our way and you'd have no complaints on that score."

"Let's not talk politics," she said wearily. "Maybe it's what you say, and I'm just naturally suspicious. I don't want to talk about it."

"Well, I was just trying to help—"

The sentence was interrupted by a monstrous explosion.

"Good God!" Shamar cried. "What was that?"

"Oh, that," Ge-Ge said, shaking off the effects. "They were probably testing one of their damned automated factories to see if it was explosion proof and it wasn't."

CHAPTER IV

During the week alone in the cabin, Ge-Ge fell in love with Shamar.

"Oh, my God!" she cried. "What will I do when they catch you? I'll die, Shamar! I couldn't bear it. We'll go to Xxla, we'll hide away as quietly as two mice, somewhere. We won't go out. The two of us, alone but together, behind closed doors and drawn shades. Nobody will ever know about us. We'll be the invisible people."

Shamar protested. "I don't see how we can ever be secure until something's done about your government. As long as you don't reach some kind of agreement with Earth, I'll be an outlaw. I'll be afraid any minute they'll tap my shoulder and come and take me away. I don't think we could hold up under that. We'd be at each other in no time."

She wept quietly.

The last day in the cabin, they went out and dug up the rest of the money. The trip to Xxla took place without incident. Ge-Ge rented an apartment for him, and he safely checked in. She went shopping for food and clothing.

Thereafter she came nearly every evening. They would eat and she would reveal the inconsequential details of the office regime to which she was daily exposed. After dinner, they would sit in the living room and practice Itraian and neck a little. Then she would go home.

One day, after a month of this routine, she threw herself into his arms and sobbed, "I gave Von Stutsman back his earring today. It was the only fair thing to do. I'm afraid he knows about us. He's had me watched. I know he has. I admitted it was another man."

Shamar held her tensely.

She broke away. "You were born in Zuleb, you suffered amnesia, you woke up in a ditch one morning without papers. You've been an itinerant worker since. Things like that happen all the time. You hit a big lottery ticket a few months ago. I told him that. How can he check it?"

"You told him I didn't have any papers?"

"Millions of people don't have any papers—the drifters, people that do casual labor, the people that don't work at all. The thing is, without papers he doesn't have any way to check on you. Oh, you should have seen his face when I gave him back his earring. He was absolutely livid. I didn't think he had it in him. I suppose I'll have to quit my job now. Oh, if you only had papers so we could be married!"

Ge-Ge's mood, that evening, alternated between despair and optimism. In the end, she was morose and restless. She repeated several times, "I just don't know what's going to happen to us."

"Ge-Ge," he said, "I can't spend my life in this apartment I've got to get out."

"You're mad." She faced him from across the room. She stood with her legs apart, firmly set. "Well, I don't care what happens any more. I can't stand things to go on like they are. I'll introduce you to some people I know, since you won't be happy until I do. But God help us!"

After approving his accent, which had improved under her tutelage, Ge-Ge took him to a party the following Saturday.

The party was held in an ill-lighted railroad flat. People congregated cross-legged on the bare floor.

Shamar listened to a man complaining that citizens were being taxed beyond all endurance to support the enforced automation program. "They aren't interested in building consumer goods. They're interested in building factories to build consumer goods and blow them up testing them. Or the factories are always obsolete just as soon as they finish them, and they can't phase into their new production setup and Hundred Year Plan."

Ge-Ge whispered a warning to him to beware of spies.

"Spies?"

"The Party," she said, drawing him to one side.

"But—but—you mean the Party just lets people talk like this?"

"Whatever harm does it do?" she asked. "Everybody benefits from talking out their aggressions. Now, have another drink and relax, and Shamar, be careful! Nobody minds local crackpots, but nobody wants *foreign* crackpots!"

She led him to another drink and left him standing with the host.

"Nice party," Shamar said.

"Thank you," the host said. "I find it very invigorating. As long as there's still people that think and that criticize on this planet, I feel there's hope, don't you? This is your first time? I don't recall your face. I have a study group that meets Wednesday nights. You're welcome to come. We have very stimulating discussions about government and politics. Please do come, any time you can. Just drop in any time after eight. What was your name again?"

"Shamar the Worker."

"Interesting name," the host said. "Another drink?"

Later, Shamar found himself in an intense conversation with a bearded youth of perhaps seventeen.

"A guy's responsible for his own conduct, right? Right! I'm responsible for *their* conduct? Each man goes to hell in his own way, right? Right! I don't want anything to do with them. You can't do anything about it, man, that's what I'm telling you. I don't seem to be getting through. Don't you see, it's a machine...."

"But if everybody joined the Party," Shamar suggested.

"So everybody joins? So what's new? Okay, you vote in the Party elections. What do you get? You get these two guys running for office: one is slightly left of center and one is slightly right of center. And both are four-square for the Automated Factory Program. Just suppose you did get a radical—suppose they accidentally let one slip through? He goes off and they argue him into line, and when he comes back, you say, 'Like, man, what happened?' And so he tells you, 'Well, I couldn't do anything about it.' That's just what I'm telling you."

"I can't see that," Shamar said. "I just don't believe that."

At another time, Shamar tried to explain free elections to a female. He was informed, "Man, just give me a way to cast a vote against all those crumbs—and then I'll think twice about all this guff you're peddling."

A sober, scholarly man told him, "Join the Party? Whatever for? You join the Party and you're expected to spend all your free evenings at rallies and meetings and speeches and in ceremonial parades in honor of the ground breaking for a new automated factory. No, thank you."

Another told him, "You need a lesson in economics, son. What do you mean by free society? The only way you can run an industrial society is to limit production. If you produce enough for everybody, the government would produce itself out of business. Look here. The Party has millions of tabulating machines of one kind or another clicking happily away day and night arranging production to fit income distribution. They've never been known to goof and produce a surplus of anything. Why, damn it, if every man, woman and child in the world went out to buy a pound of nails apiece, the shortage of nails would be fantastic. But would they produce more nails? You know they wouldn't. 'So you want more nails?' they'd say. 'Well, damn you, work for them!' And the price would go up. See what I mean, son? They'd have another stick to beat us with."

Later, Shamar found himself seated on the floor across from an aesthetic in his late thirties. "You see, my friend, force and violence never accomplish their stated ends. We must stand firmly on the principle of non-violence."

"But that's taking it laying down," Shamar protested.

"No! Sometimes I think it goes to the very core of human existence. Perhaps this is the central import of all philosophy: the way things are done is more important than the ends that are obtained."

At that point, Ge-Ge arrived breathlessly. "Shamar, quickly! We must go!"

"Huh? I'm having this interesting little talk—"

She tugged him from the floor. Baffled, he followed her. As he did so, the fighting broke out in the far corner of the room.

"Quickly!" she said. "Let's get out of here before the police come."

They fought their way, hand in hand, to the door. There they paused for a moment to look back.

"It's a couple of rival socialist parties fighting," she explained breathlessly.

"What about?"

"God knows. Hurry."

They were in the street. "Don't run, walk," she cautioned. After a block, she said, "I didn't even need to watch you at the end. Everybody got so drunk nobody noticed you much."

"Even the spies?"

"Oh, they always get the drunkest."

The siren sounded.

"Let's hurry."

When they arrived at Shamar's apartment, she asked, "Well, what did you think of the party?"

"It was an education," he said after a moment.

CHAPTER V

The following week Shamar spent many hours walking the streets of Xxla. He tried to convince himself that the people he had met at the party were not representative.

They were.

Friday night Ge-Ge announced "Shamar, I can't stand much more of this! What's going to happen? What is Von Stutsman going to do? He's onto something. I sometimes wish—oh, God!—I sometimes wish something would happen so we'd know where we stand, so we'd know what to do!" He tried to put an arm around her, but she brushed it away. "Don't! Let me alone!"

She retired to the other side of the room. For a moment, and for no reason, the hostility in the air between them was like ice and fire.

"I'm sorry," Ge-Ge said curtly.

"That's all right," Shamar said, his voice cold and distant.

"Let's talk about something else."

They were silent for a minute. Then he said, "I wanted to ask you. Of all the people I talked to, I couldn't find anyone who seemed to give a damn, one way or the other, about Earth. Why is that? You'd think they'd be at least talking about Earth."

"Why should they be? We've got our own problems."

At that point, the police arrived and took Shamar the Worker away.

They put him in a cell in which there were already three other prisoners.

"What you in for, buddy?"

Shamar studied the prisoner for a moment without answering. His companions looked up.

"No visible means of support," Shamar said.

"I'm Long John Freed."

Shamar nodded.

"They're trying to hook you for evading the productivity tax, huh?"

Shamar declined comment.

Freed settled back on his bunk. "I say take them for all you can. Now, look, you're a little guy. So they bleed us white. Take a factory manager or an important Black Market operator—you think they pay taxes? You can bet they don't. It's a racket. The poor pay and pay because they can't hire fancy lawyers to lie for them; and the rich take and take. I don't see why the Party puts up with it."

Freed shifted his position. "Say what you will about the Party—and I know it's got it's faults—still, there are dedicated men in it. I may be a small-time crook, but I'm as patriotic as the next man. The Party's done a lot of good.

"First time for you? How old are you, twenty-seven or so? First time, they usually try to recruit you for the Factory Force.

"It's not such a bad racket. When you start out, they toss you in with lots of kids—usually the draftees. You get six weeks pick-and-shovel, and you're really dragging when you finish that. Then comes specialist school.

"Try to get in as an electrician or plumber. Plasterers or bricklayers have to work too hard. Carpentry's not bad—I'd hold out for cabinet-making, rather than rough carpentry, if I had to go into that. Then there's real specialties. Tile laying. You have to have a personality for that, or you'd go nuts. Demolition's not too bad; you blow up obsolete factories. That would have been right down my alley."

Freed was silent a moment, then he resumed:

"Sometimes I may talk like a radical, and maybe I am a little of a radical, I don't know. You look at the overall picture, things ain't too bad. I've known a lot of thieves and petty crooks in my time. As a class, for pure patriotism, I'll stack them up against anybody you can name; and in a way, you know, I'm kind of proud of that.... Well, let's shut up and get some shut-eye."

When finally he slept, Shamar dreamed that the Party was a vast, invulnerable pyramid resting on the shifting base of the population. It was constructed to dampen out vibrations. The bottom quivered, and the quiver ran upward a few inches and was absorbed. The top of the pyramid remained stable, fixed and motionless, indifferent even to its own foundation. The pyramid was built like an earthquake-proof tower. It was built to last. The Party was built to govern. It need only devote itself to its own preservation. Any other issue was secondary.

It was an organic machine. The gears were flesh and blood. The people on top were maintenance engineers. Their job was to go around with an oil can that they could squirt when necessary to keep friction to a minimum.

He awakened the following morning ravenously hungry and was hugely disappointed by breakfast. Even discounting his somewhat biased viewpoint, the food was inedible.

Freed accepted Shamar's share eagerly with the comment, "It'll taste better after you miss a few meals. It always does."

An hour later, the jailer came to open the cell.

"Shamar the Worker? Get your stuff. We're going."

Ge-Ge was waiting in the reception room. Her hair had been especially waved for the occasion. She wore a suit newly pressed and gleaming. She had tears in her eyes.

She fled to his arms. "Darling!" she cried, caressing his face with childlike wonder. "Was it awful? Did they beat you?"

"I'm fine."

"Darling, we're going to get you out on bail. I've made all the arrangements. We just have to go to the Judge's chambers for a minute, and they'll let you go. Thank God you're going to be out of this horrible place, at least for a little while."

The jailer brought Shamar's belt and his bag of possessions. Shamar signed a receipt for them and they went to the Judge.

The Judge said, "Please be seated." He had a resonant and friendly voice. He went to his desk and sat down.

Ge-Ge and Shamar seated themselves before him.

"Ah, you young people," he said. "Now, you must be Shamar the Worker, and you—"

"Garfling Germadpoldlt."

"Of course." He turned to Shamar. "I hate to see a fine young person like you in trouble, Shamar. It seems to me such a waste. Man and boy, for sixty years I've been a dedicated worker for the Party. Oh, Shamar, when I think of that glorious paradise to come—that time of wealth and plenty for all—that time when the riches and abundance of Mother Itra will, from Automation, overflow alike the homes of the rich and poor...."

They waited.

He continued. "Here I sit, year after year, Garfling and Shamar, judging my fellow men. Judging poor creatures who do not live the Dream. I sometimes feel that this is not the way. I sometimes feel my job is out there on the street corners, preaching the Dream, awakening the souls, telling the story of love and beauty and abundance in the life to come.

"Ah, me. But the world is not yet perfect, is it? And man's understanding is imperfect. Here you are before me today, Shamar, with no visible means of support and no record of having paid productivity taxes. Oh, what a grim and fearful picture! In all your life have you ever once thought of your obligation to the future? You have failed yourself; you have failed the Party; and failed the future.

"Yet—in a larger sense—although this in no way militates against your own guilt—have we not failed you? How have we permitted a human soul to degrade himself to the point where we must punish him?"

Abruptly, the Judge stood up. "Well, I've done the best I can. I remand you to the custody of Miss Germadpoldlt. Your trial will be set at a later date. You are not to leave Xxla without permission of this court. And I hope my lecture today has fallen on fertile soil. It is not too late to correct your ways. And I may say, if I am the one who hears your case, your conduct between now and the trial may have some bearing on the outcome."

They took a taxi back to his apartment. Ge-Ge trembled violently most of the way and nestled against him; they murmured their affection.

After he had been fed, she said nervously, "It was Von Stutsman who was responsible for your arrest. I should have known we couldn't fight the Party. If he digs hard enough, nothing on Itra can save us."

Finally, she went out to canvas lawyers.

She came back at dusk.

"Shamar, darling," she said, "I've located him. I asked a lot of my friends, and he's the best. He's a big lawyer for left-wing people. I talked to him, I told him everything."

"What! You told him everything?"

"Why, yes."

"You, you told him I was an Earthman?" He grabbed her by the shoulders. "Listen, Ge-Ge! I was arrested on a charge I could beat; now look what you've done. What makes you think he won't turn me over to the Party? This is too big, now! This isn't just a tax avoidance matter, this is treason for him."

"It's all right, darling," she said soothingly, breaking free from him. "I had to tell him so he'd take the case. Why would a big man like him want to defend a common vagrant?"

Shamar closed his mouth. "But—you mean, he won't tell anyone?"

"Of course not."

"Has the man no patriotism?"

"Look, Shamar," she said in exasperation, "you once asked me why the people in the street aren't upset about Earth. I'm beginning to see the way you think. What you mean is, aren't we *afraid* of Earth? Aren't we afraid Earth would, oh, do something like invade us or something? That's what you mean."

"Of course it is."

"Once upon a time," she said, "when we first got space flight, the Party got all shook up about the possibility of some hostile force out there developing an interstellar drive and coming along and doing their will with us. They asked the computers about it. Invading and conquering a planet is such a vast technological undertaking that the mind just boggles at it. Don't forget, we've got a warning network out there. They're not very alert, or you wouldn't have gotten through, but they wouldn't miss an invasion fleet. There's computer-controlled chemical rockets in orbit, and we've got a few sited on Itra that can blast down anything that slows up to try to land. It wouldn't take one-hundredth, it wouldn't take one-thousandth of the technological resources required to defend Itra that it would to attack her. Earth just simply can't afford to attack us. They'd go broke trying. Every million dollars you spent to get here, we'd spend a thousand to keep you from landing.

"Oh, I suppose if Earth wanted to, they might figure out some way to blow up Itra. But where's the profit in that? We're not bothering you. Why spend all that money when it's not going to get you one damn thing in return?"

The following day, Shamar called on the lawyer, Counselor Freemason.

Counselor Freemason inquired politely as to the state of his financial reserves. Shamar replied reassuringly.

"Good, good. That's most encouraging. Most encouraging indeed. We need not place any limit on our ingenuity, then.

"I've been thinking about your case, Mr. Worker. The thing first to do, in my opinion, is to stir up public sympathy in your favor. It's almost an ideal case. It has no real political overtones. It's not as if you're accused of anything serious. Well, I believe I can interest some friends of mine who are always deeply concerned with cases involving the infringement of an individual's liberty—provided, of course, there are no political overtones. I can think of several good people who would be willing to head up a Defense Committee. The fact that we have and I'm talking now about as much as, oh, one hundred thousand dollars?" He paused interrogatively.

"I'm prepared to pay," Shamar said.

"Maybe even more," Councilman Freemason continued quickly. "We can come to that later. The important thing right now is to get down to work on your case."

"Counselor Freemason, now, obviously I'm not a lawyer," Shamar said, "and I know it's bad business to tell a professional how to run his job. But I believe Miss Germadpoldlt explained the, ah, rather unusual delicacy of my own position. It would seem to me that the less publicity we got, the better."

Counselor Freemason shook a pen at him. "A very good point, Mr. Worker. It shows you're thinking, and I'm glad of the opportunity to explain the reasons for this recommendation. If I brazenly parade you before them, you see, by implication it means we're not afraid of your background being examined. We have nothing to hide. Consequently, they will not look for anything. If, on the other hand, I'm cautious, fearful, defensive, they'll ask themselves, 'What's Counselor Freemason trying to hide?' And they'll start digging into your past.

"Now, I hope that clears that matter up to your satisfaction? Good. Good. I'll get right to work on your case. Do you have anything else? Miss Germadpoldlt explained rather nicely, I think, yesterday. As far as anyone knows, you're a man without papers. You've never paid any taxes but they have no proof you owe taxes. You won money in the lottery. You collected anonymously; lots of people do for perfectly valid reasons. Let them prove you didn't win. The Party can't be very interested in a man like that.

"So, I'll raise an issue. Maybe we'll suggest that any lottery winner is likely to be persecuted. The Party wants things to go smoothly. The lottery makes the people feel as if, you know, they actually own a piece of things. And too many people don't have papers.

"My job is to take the specific and convert it to a vague general principle that a number of people feel deeply about. The Party will take the easy way out: they're not dumb. They've learned from experience. You're not worth that much trouble to them. Otherwise, there'll be a period of aggravation, people without papers beating up police and things like that."

Three days later, Shamar met with the newly formed Committee of One Hundred for Justice to Shamar the Worker.

There were five members of the Committee and Counselor Freemason in attendance. They briefed him on their initial activities.

They had printed letterheads and were circulating letters to people known to be friendly, with a hastily printed booklet giving the facts of the case.

"As you can see," Counselor Freemason said, "we're off to a very fast start. Um, the question naturally arises as to finances. I have advanced a certain amount out of my own pocket.... We will need more than I can conveniently scrape together at the moment, and I'm reluctant to—ah—impose on the Committee for a loan insofar as—"

"I took the liberty of bringing along some cash," Shamar said. "For current expenses and, of course, your retainer."

They looked relieved. "Excellent, excellent. I might suggest, Mr. Worker, that we appoint one of the Committee as treasurer—perhaps Mrs. Freetle, here—" the lady smiled—"to take these financial worries off your mind. This will leave you free to devote yourself fully to activities defense."

"Now that that's out of the way," one of the male Committee members said, "let's get right down to business. As you can see, we're moving fast. Our overall strategy is this. We must first establish a public image for you, Mr. Worker, an image the average man can identify with. Counselor Freemason has described your case to us. I simply don't know what the Party's coming to to permit a man like Von Stutsman to persecute you this way. Oh, I tell you, it makes my blood boil, Mr. Worker!"

Others of the Committee chimed in and the sentiment passed heatedly among them.

"Well," said Counselor Freemason, "I guess that about winds it up for the moment. You all know where to reach me. Any time, day or night. I guess, Mr. Worker, if you'll just turn the money over to Mrs. Freetle. And I think, Mr. Hall, if you'd hire that speech writer—what's his name? McGoglhy?—to work with Mr. Worker on his speeches."

"Speeches?" Shamar asked.

"You're going to be our featured speaker at all the rallies, of course," Mrs. Freetle said. "I know you will do splendidly, just splendidly! Your accent is so captivating. I've never heard anything quite like it."

CHAPTER VI

On the evening of his first public appearance, Shamar was given a neatly typed speech. He rehearsed it hurriedly, stammers and all.

"Fellow citizens! As I stand here, looking over this sea of faces, hearing your applause and seeing how your hearts go out to one poor man in distress, it—I—Well, I'm deeply touched. I can't tell you how much it means to me. I prepared a speech for tonight, but I'm not going to use it. I'm just going to stand here, instead, and tell you, just as the words come out, how I feel." Here he would pause for applause and then continue. "Thank you so very much. Thank you. I know you're all behind me—except for the police agents in the audience." Here he would wait for laughter. "We all know them, don't we? I see about a dozen. A dozen agents have come down here to find out what I'm going to say. Isn't that ridiculous?" Here there would be mixed laughter, applause and cries in the affirmative. "All right! Thank you. I hope they get an earful tonight."

Later in the speech he would demand, "Why are they doing this to me? I want you to tell me why. What have I done? What am I accused of doing? Well, I'll tell you this—I'm not the kind of a man who is going to submit meekly to this persecution. I'm going to fight back. I've got a little money left from my lottery winnings, and I'll spend every cent of it to fight these people doing this thing to me." Here he would pause dramatically. "I want to leave you with this point. It's not just Shamar the Worker that's involved. What am I? A poor, itinerant laborer going from town to town. I'm nothing, I have never had anything, and I guess I never will have anything. I'm no rich black marketeer or businessman. I'm no fat politician. I'm just one little man. But it's not me—and this is the point I want to leave you with—it's not Shamar the Worker. He's unimportant. What is important is that if they can do this to me, they can do it to you. If they can do it to Shamar the Worker today, next year one of you will be up here on this platform speaking just the way I am. So you see, this is your fight. It's not me that's important—it's the principle that's important—"

The meeting went brilliantly. Every time he paused, the audience responded just as the speech-writer had indicated. It was as if they were as well rehearsed as he.

The next night, another meeting. And another. And another. He slept no more than four hours a night when the campaign was in full swing. He spoke dozens of times into the bright glare of TV cameras. He paraded down a million streets in an open-topped car. Faces poured in front of his own; on and on they came. People with tears in their eyes cried, "God bless Shamar the Worker!" Once the Committee hired a brass band.

So, for two weeks, it went.

Then the Party threw him back in jail, in an apparent effort to deprive the movement of its momentum.

After three days, during which time Shamar was held incommunicado, Counselor Freemason obtained permission to interview his client.

"We're making marvelous progress! Ge-Ge is turning into a most effective crusader. You should hear her when she cries, 'Give me back my man!' This is a wonderful development for us. It's having the opposite of the intended effect. Von Stutsman has over-reached himself this time. The Party is going to have to back down, and it will cost him dearly."

"How's the finances?"

"Ge-Ge has given us some advances—"

"How much have you spent?"

"Well, to tell you the truth, I haven't been keeping track closely. Perhaps we've run a little more than we anticipated. The response, you see—"

Shamar returned to his cell wishing Earth's printing presses had worked a little longer.

It took nearly two weeks to arrange for Ge-Ge to visit him. When she arrived, she was nearly on the point of tears.

"Oh, my darling, how I've missed you!"

She brought him up to date on the progress of his case. As Counselor Freemason had reported, his imprisonment merely increased the vigor of his supporters. Now they were at their highest pitch: a pitch which would be difficult to maintain.

"I'm just worried sick," she said. "If the Party can hold out another week or two. I don't want to worry you, Shamar, but I want you to know how you stand. Counselor Freemason says the worst that could happen would be a short prison sentence, no more than a year, for not filing tax forms. We could keep you out on appeal for quite a while."

"Ge-Ge, how much have we spent so far?"

"About three hundred thousand dollars."

"Good God! They'll have it all when they get through! If I ever get back to Earth—"

"I don't care about money, Shamar! I just want you free!"

He took her shoulders. "Ge-Ge, suppose the Party can't afford to back down? Maybe they feel they have to stand firm to prevent a lot of future trouble. And when Freemason gets all the money ... then what chance will we stand? They might railroad me for years. They'll make an example out of me. Now, are you willing to gamble? Everybody would jump at the chance to vote them out. If we could—"

"Please, Shamar," Ge-Ge said. "All this voting thing you've always been so sold on is all right, I guess—but it just won't work. To begin with, there isn't any way to vote."

"Maybe there is," he said.

Shamar was still in jail the following day when Ge-Ge appeared on the TV program.

PAMDEN had been reluctant to release time to her. PAMDEN was Itra's largest industrial co-operative—Plastics, Agricultural Machinery, Detergents, Electricity and Newsprint—and, being the most efficient, was responsible for operating the TV networks.

"Good heavens," said the station executive. "Nobody can say we haven't already given you coverage. Miss Germadpoldlt."

"They've ordered you to stop!" she protested.

"They? The Party? Miss Germadpoldlt, do you honestly believe that? Nobody tells a station manager what to program. Believe me. There is no prior censorship whatsoever. But, on the other hand, we can't turn over the TV stations to minority propaganda either."

Ge-Ge argued and pleaded, and in the end the executive sighed wearily. "I think we've been more than fair. But for you—and this is a personal favor, Miss Germadpoldlt, because you are a young and attractive woman—for you, I will phone our program director and see if he can get you on the Noon Interview Show for tomorrow. It gives you the Itra-wide network, which is certainly more than anyone has the right to ask. You'll have ninety seconds to make your case. That's the best I can do."

"Oh, thank you, thank you," Ge-Ge sobbed. "You're so fair and generous." Outside his office she took a deep breath, crossed her fingers and went home to revise her speech. She had only expected sixty.

Ge-Ge arrived at the studio well in advance and was handed over to the makeup department. With deft skill they converted her youth to age and contrived to instill in her face weariness and defeat. Her protests were ignored.

"This is the way you make up for TV," she was told.

They clucked collective tongues in disapproval when they were finished and sent her on her way to a brief chat with the M.C.

The M.C. assured her that she looked divine and hastily scanned her prepared remarks, which had been heavily edited by some anonymous hand in the news department. The M.C. incorporated a few pointless revisions and dispatched the message to the department handling idiot-board material. It was explained that Ge-Ge was to read, word for word, from the electronic prompter.

Ge-Ge watched the program from the wings. When she heard a commercial message in favor of the consumption of a particular variety of candy, her heart ran away with itself. Her courage faltered. But Shamar's face brought it back.

The signal came. She walked into the terrible glare which held up every imperfection to microscopic inspection. She shook hands, turned, and the camera closed in, full face. Beyond the camera lay the largest daytime TV audience on Itra. She felt they were examining her pores with minute and critical attention.

She blinked nervously and began to read. "I am here to tell you about Shamar the Worker." That was as far as she went with the prepared text. Before the horrified ears of the auditors in the studio, she plunged into remarks of another kind entirely.

"If you want to do something to help Shamar the Worker, stop buying candy! Don't buy any more candy. If you want to help Shamar the Worker, don't buy any candy until he's free. If you want to help Shamar, please, *please*, don't buy—"

At this point the technicians cut Ge-Ge out and, with profound mistiming, faded in an oleogenous taped message from the candy manufacturer which began, "Friends, everybody likes Red Block candy, and millions buy it every day. Here's why—"

Ge-Ge surveyed the surrounding confusion and walked unmolested from the studio.

When she arrived home, an angry Counselor Freemason was waiting on her doorstep. Inside, she allowed the Counselor to present his case.

This new move, he explained, would have terrible consequences. Shamar's good faith would be prejudiced. One simply did not, with impunity, go outside the law in such matters. There were rules you absolutely *must* play the game by. He washed his hands of all responsibility for her conduct. "I hope to God nothing comes of it," he concluded. "I'm having the Committee prepare a denial of—"

The phone rang at this point, and without asking permission, Counselor Freemason answered it. "Yes? This is Counselor Freemason, go ahead." He listened a moment, said, "They did," in a weary voice and cradled the phone.

He turned to Ge-Ge. "Now we're in for it. That was Pete Freedle from the Committee."

"Well," said Ge-Ge, "I think we'll just wait a few days and see what happens."

A week later, Ge-Ge was still waiting. Counselor Freemason, deprived of finances, was powerless to move. He saw everything crashing in shambles at their feet.

"But are they selling candy?" Ge-Ge asked.

"That's beside the point!" Counselor Freemason cried. "Look here, every crackpot on the planet will get into the act. They don't care about Shamar. All you're going to prove now is that the Party is unpopular. Everyone already knows that." He struck his forehead in exasperation.

For two weeks, all was quiet. There were no more rallies for Shamar the Worker. Signs were torn down and destroyed. No bulletins were printed. No word passed over the electronic communications network. The Committee, bankrupt, dissolved in mutual recriminations and bickering, convinced that the cause of civil liberties had been set back one hundred years.

But candy was not selling.

It clogged the distribution channels. It piled up in warehouses. It lay untouched in stores. It grew rancid. Mechanically the factories continued to turn it out.

The Party denied the boycott was having any effect. This did not appease the distributors of candy and the sellers of candy and the producers of candy. Their jobs were at stake. They had payrolls to meet.

The Party stopped production of candy. People suddenly found themselves with no jobs to go to.

The economic system was so tightly controlled and organized that the effect was immediate. There was too little money available to purchase the supplies normally purchased. Suppliers cut back on their factory orders. This further reduced the need for supplies.

At this point, the Party decided that the people would, by heaven, eat candy. The Party Leader himself went on TV to appeal to the patriotism of the people and to order them to resume buying candy. This was a tactical error. But being the idea of the Party Leader himself, who had always crashed headlong into obstacles, none opposed it.

The issue was directly joined. People resented being told that it was their patriotic duty to eat something that all medical opinion held was harmful. Furthermore, people realized that they had somehow stumbled on a fatal flaw in the system, which they could exploit without immediate danger.

They responded by refusing to buy soap.

The people were now in open revolt. At last they had a method for disapproving of things in general.

The economy plummeted. The computers were in a frenzy. Effects of corrective actions were no longer predictable. The Party frantically tried to buy soap and dump it. The people turned to other commodities.

Pressure now mounted from within the Party itself. The Supervisor of PAMDEN saw his carefully nurtured empire begin to disintegrate. A massive layoff in Consumer Plastics (badly hit by a running boycott) took with it valuable key personnel. The Supervisor of PAMDEN told the Party Leader himself that he damned well better do something about the situation, and damned soon, too.

The Party Leader himself ordered the release of Shamar the Worker.

But by then no one was interested in Shamar the Worker.

The man came and unlocked Shamar's cell door. Shamar stood up. The guard tossed in Shamar's clothing. "Get dressed." Shamar got dressed. "Come along." Shamar came along.

Shamar had had no word from outside for nearly two months, and it was not until he saw Ge-Ge's face, radiant with joy, that he realized he had won.

"You're free!" she cried excitedly.

Shamar was given back his belt and possessions. As they waited for the Judge to make it official, Shamar asked, "I wonder what will happen now?"

"Nobody knows. Everybody says the Party's out for sure. Individual Party members will try to form a new government, but it's going to have to be radically different. They'll try to keep all they can, but the people will wring them dry for every last concession. Maybe now when they build the factories, they'll stay built and actually produce something."

"For a little while," Shamar said.

"Longer than a little while," Ge-Ge said. "We've got a way to vote now, when things get too bad."

The Judge, in his red robe, came in. They stood respectfully. He looked at them for a long time and said nothing. Finally, he spoke:

"Well, Shamar the Worker, I guess you've got what you want. You pulled down a whole civilization. I hope you're satisfied. What Dream will you give us to replace the Dream you have taken from us?"

His face hardened.

"Shamar the Worker," he said, "the Party Leader himself has asked us to dismiss the pending charges against you. This I now do. You are free to go."

"Thank you, sir," Shamar said respectfully.

"Shamar the Worker, for your own sake, you better hope that I never see you in my court. You better not get yourself arrested for anything. I will show you no mercy, but justice will be swift and summary. So that you may not rest easily at night, I am having some of my very skillful and competent friends check through your background thoroughly. You should hope, very sincerely, that they find nothing. You may go."

Ge-Ge and Shamar stood. They turned in silence. When they were at the door, the Judge called, "Oh, Shamar the Worker!"

He turned, "Yes, sir?"

"Shamar the Worker, I do not like your accent."

Shamar could feel Ge-Ge trembling uncontrollably at his side.

But when they reached the street, they were greeted by headlines announcing that a delegation from the planet Earth had arrived.

CHAPTER VII

The Earth delegation had taken over a suite in the Party Hotel, grandest and most expensive on Itra. Usually it was reserved for high Party members.

Shamar and Ge-Ge presented themselves at the desk. Shamar wrote out a note in English. "Deliver this to the Earthmen," he instructed.

Shamar and Ge-Ge retired to await results. Less than five minutes passed; the bell hop returned. "Sir and Madam," he said respectfully, "come with me."

When he entered the suite, he felt the personality of Shamar the Worker drop from him into memory.

"Captain Shaeffer! Captain Shaeffer! Oh, what a magnificent job! I'm Gene Gibson from the new Department of Extra-Terrestrial Affairs. Who's this?"

"This is my fiancee."

"Good heavens, man, you intend to marry a *native*?" The man stepped back, shocked.

Capt. Shaeffer turned to Ge-Ge and performed bilingual introductions.

They moved from the hallway to the sitting room and arranged themselves on the furniture.

"I must say, Captain Shaeffer, that your success on Itra has surpassed our wildest expectations. The first inkling we had was when, out of the blue, as it were, there was your face looking out at us from the TV screen! You should have been there for our celebration that night! You'd been on Itra just a little over two months! You're going down in history as one of the greatest heroes of all time!"

Capt. Shaeffer said, "I think it would be best if Ge-Ge and I were to board your ship immediately. Her life may be in danger. Some old-line Party men might resent her role in the revolution. Actually, she had more to do with it than I did."

"Oh, now, I'm sure you must be exaggerating a bit on that, Captain Shaeffer. Her life in danger? Surely, now! Speaking frankly, Captain—and mind you, I have no personal objection at all; this is none of my business. But she is, after all, an *Itraian*. You know these mixed marriages—"

"I don't give a damn what you personally think," Capt. Shaeffer said. "Is that understood once and for all? She goes."

"Of course. I was just—now don't get huffy. Of course she goes. Just as you wish, Captain."

The angry exchange over an unknown but fearfully expected issue caused Ge-Ge to blink back tears.

A week later, Gene Gibson came for the first time to visit them. Capt. Shaeffer inquired as to progress.

"Well, Captain, things are progressing. We are establishing a government which will be more responsive to the will of the people of Itra. We've had several very pleasant, informal chats with the Party Leader, himself. Really a wonderful man. Once he got all the facts—which were kept from him the first time we landed—he strikes me as being quite responsible. I think we may have misjudged him. I'm not too sure but what he isn't just the exact man to head up the new government. We've discussed a few details on trade agreements and, I must say, he's been very reasonable."

Capt. Shaeffer said nothing.

"Yes," Gene Gibson said, "he's really an exceptional individual. A wealth of administrative experience. A fine grasp of practical politics. I don't regard him as a typical Itraian at all. He feels that, with us backing him, we can get this whole mess straightened out in a few months."

"Mess?"

"Well, you must admit, I think, Captain Shaeffer, that you did—well—make negotiations extremely difficult, in view of the, ah, present temper of the populace.

"You see, Earth would like to have a stable and responsible government. A government, that is, which can see larger issues in perspective. Not one which must devote its full time to coping with a group of unpatriotic anarchists running loose in the streets."

"What's he saying?" Ge-Ge asked.

"As it is now," Gene Gibson continued, "we do have several rather difficult problems. I think we'll probably have to quarantine Itra for a few months until the Party Leader himself can form a stable organizational structure. Somehow news of our trade discussions have leaked out and for some reason has resulted in a general work stoppage. So you see? By God, I'll just come right out and say it: Shaeffer, you've left us one hell of a mess!"

With that, Gene Gibson departed.

"What did he say?" Ge-Ge asked meekly. But Shaeffer only shook his head.

The following day, the ship's captain came to pay a courtesy call.

"A very neat piece of work, Merle. Your new assignment just came in, by the way, on the space radio."

"New assignment? Ge-Ge and I are on our way back to Earth."

"No, you're not. We're to drop you off at Midway for transhipment to Folger's Hill. It's a new planet. You're to be Earth representative to the people of Folger's Hill. The first shipload of colonists arrived about a month ago."

"I see," Capt. Shaeffer said.

"The salary's good," the ship's captain said.

"Suppose I don't want to go?"

"I've got orders to leave you at Midway. I'd want to go if I were you. They want you out of the way for a little while. You can't fight it. You've been appointed a General in the Defense Forces, so you're now under military law—and it's an order."

At this point, Ge-Ge broke in to say, "How are things going in Xxla?"

General Shaeffer choked back his anger and presented the question.

"They don't tell us anything. The crew is confined to the ship."

Shamar the Worker turned to Ge-Ge. "It's going about the same," he said.

A year later, General Merle S. Shaeffer's card popped out of the computer.

"General Shaeffer's up for re-assignment."

"Who in hell is General Shaeffer?"

"Never heard of him."

The card passed upward.

"Merle Shaeffer is due for re-assignment," a man who knew the name told the Secretary of the Over Council at lunch the following day. "There's a new planet opened up even further away than Folger's Hill."

"He's the one who butchered the Itra assignment? Send him there. Anything new from Itra recently, by the way?"

"Same as usual. I understand the anarchists have formed some kind of government."

"Terrible. Terrible. Well, the less said about that the better."

A week later, again over lunch, the Secretary was told:

"I guess we needn't worry about Merle Shaeffer any more. Disappeared from his post, he and that Itraian woman of his, a couple of weeks after they arrived on Folger's Hill. Probably a hunting accident got them both. Their bodies were never found. These things happen on wild new planets."

The Secretary was silent for a long time. Then he said: "Shaeffer dead, eh? I guess it's better that way. Well, a genius has passed, and we'll not see his like again. Perverted, perhaps, but a genius none the less."

They drank solemnly.

"To Merle Shaeffer. You could call him a hero, so let's you and I drink to that. No one else ever will."

They drank again.

Nothing further served to stir the Secretary's memory of Merle Shaeffer, and he retired six months later at the end of his term. The new Secretary was not familiar with the Itraian affair.

He had been in office just a few days less than a year when, one morning, he arrived at his office in a furious rage. "Get me the Head of the Defense Forces!"

"I'm sorry, sir, all the phones are tied up," his secretary said.

"What in hell do you mean, all the phones are tied up?"

"I don't know. Maybe all at once everybody just left their phones off the hook or something."

"Why would they do that? That's ridiculous! Get a runner over after him."

Half an hour later, the Head of the Defense Forces arrived.

"Do you know," the new Secretary demanded, "that yesterday all the pennies went out of circulation? People apparently have been saving them for the last couple of months. It finally showed up. All at once, there aren't any pennies. You can't make change. Damn it, why would those crazy idiots all decide to save their pennies at the same time? It's not rational. Why did they do it?"

The Head of the Defense Forces said nothing.

The Secretary raved at him in anger, but the Head of the Defense Forces did not have the heart to tell him that a hero had returned home.